The Kite Runner

by Khaled Hosseini

A Study Guide by Ray Moore

Acknowledgements:
Where I have selectively quoted from the writings of others in the course of my own argument, I have done so in the sincere belief that this constitutes Fair Use. I will immediately remove any quotation if requested to do so.

Contents

The Kite Runner by Khaled Hosseini

Introduction

Plot Summary:

This is the story of two half-brothers who grow up together as playmates in Afghanistan and whose lives become entwined in tragic ways. Baba (no other name is given) is a highly successful businessman in Kabul: Amir is his legitimate son whose mother died in childbirth; Hassan is his illegitimate son conceived during an affair between Baba and the wife of his servant Ali, a fact which has been kept a closely guarded secret. Shortly after his birth, Hassan's mother ran out on the family, so both boys grow up without the love of a mother.

Amir is an excellent competitive kite flyer and Hassan is the greatest kite runner in Kabul. (Kite runners attempt to capture the downed kites as victory trophies.) After one important kite battle that Amir wins, he witnesses his friend Hassan being attacked by three of the neighborhood boys, one of whom rapes him. Amir stands by and does nothing because he is too scared to intervene. He then has his former friend sent away by Baba on a false charge of theft, but he will feel the guilt of his cowardice and his lie for the rest of his life.

Baba and Amir emigrate from Afghanistan to California where Amir gets married and begins to make a career as a novelist. When he returns to Afghanistan, he finds that Hassan is dead but that his son, Sohrab, needs protection. Perhaps now he will be able to atone for his failure to save Hassan.

Why Read this Book?

Khaled Hosseini's first novel was well received when it was published and popular with readers. It will appeal to those of any nationality who are first- or second-generation immigrants to the U.S.A. and to readers who want to find out more about the experience of Muslims in America.

Other themes (what it means to be a father, response to bullying and terror, conscience, etc.) are universal.

Important: Issues with this Book.

The novel was clearly written for an adult audience, but having said that it contains no bad language. Of course, there is the rape of Hassan. I would certainly not call the description graphic, but it is clear what is happening. Later, it is clear that Hassan's son is also being sexually abused, though the abuse is never described.

Works Cited

"An Interview with Khaled Hosseini." *Book Browse*, 2007. Web. July 24, 2015.

Hosseini, Khaled. *The Kite Runner.* 1st Edition. New York: Riverhead Books, 2003. Print.

Ruppersburg, Hugh and Tim Engles. *Critical Essays on Don DeLillo.* First edition. New York: G. K. Hall & Co., 2000. Print.

SparkNotes Editors. "SparkNote on White Noise." *SparkNotes.com.* SparkNotes LLC. 2005. Web. 10 Jun. 2015.

A Note on the graphic organizers: Two graphic organizers are provided to enable the students to make notes. Some simple guidance will be needed depending on how the teacher wants them to be used.

Map of Afghanistan

(Author: UN Office for the Coordination of Humanitarian Affairs [OCHA]. This file is licensed under the Creative Commons Attribution 3.0 Unported license. Source: Wikipedia.)

A Study Guide

Dramatis Personæ
Spoiler alert!
If you are reading the novel for the first time, you may wish to go straight to the Study Questions and come back to this section later.

Amir's family and childhood acquaintances:
Baba (ethnicity Pashtun and religion Shi'a) - The father of Amir and Hassan is a highly successful businessman in Kabul. Although he is a Muslim, he distrusts religious fundamentalism. Nevertheless, he lives by his own strict moral code which he wishes to pass on to Amir. Baba is a determined man who has complete confidence in his own ability; he is also a brave man who is prepared to risk his life to protect others. He is often kind and generous and does a great deal of public good, such as building and financing an orphanage in Kabul. Many of his moral actions are motivated by his desire to atone for his sin in begetting Hassan, and for his failure to go against the customs of Afghanistan by acknowledging the boy as his own. Because he cannot bring himself to love Hassan openly, Baba does so with acts of kindness and generosity to the boy (such as paying for his cleft lip to be surgically repaired), but Baba's guilt makes him rather harsh on his legitimate son Amir since he is equally (though for different reasons) unable to show the boy that he loves him.

Sofia Akrami - Amir's mother died giving birth to him which is a guilt that Amir carries throughout his life. Amir knows very little about her except that she loved literature - a trait that he inherits from her.

Amir - The narrator and the protagonist of the story is a novelist living in California. He begins the story of his childhood in Afghanistan in December 2001, approximately three months after the terrorist attacks on September 11th on the Twin Towers and the Pentagon. Amir is the son of a rich and influential businessman who owns a large house in an affluent part of Kabul. Living in an adjacent hut are Ali and his son Hassan (ethnicity Hazaras and religion Sunnis). Amir and Hassan play together most of the time: Hassan is devoted to his friend, but Amir cannot overcome the social and religious gulf between the two.

Amir desperately wants his father's affection and approval, so whenever Hassan receives signs of affection from Baba, he feels bitterly jealous. Amir is one of the best kite fighters in Kabul, and Hassan is undoubtedly the best kite runner. However, Amir's first victory in a kite fighting tournament leads to an incident that will end his friendship with Hassan and leave him with a terrible burden of guilt. The novel is about Amir's attempts to atone for his failure to protect Hassan and for the lie he told to drive Hassan and Ali away.

Soraya - In her teens, Amir's wife rebelled against the strong-willed traditionalism of her father, General Taheri, and ran off with a man. The General eventually brought her home by force, which she resented at the time but for which she was ultimately grateful. Having lost her reputation, it seems unlikely that any man will want to marry her until Amir falls in love with her. She is the most Westernized Afghan character in the novel and resents the way women are treated in Afghan culture. As a wife, she is personally strong but also endlessly supportive of Amir.

Rahim Khan - Rahim is Baba's closest friend, and teacher. Amir regards him as a second father, one able to demonstrate affection in a way that Baba finds it impossible to do. Rahim knows that Baba is Amir's father but keeps his friend's secret. He also learns the truth of Amir's cowardly betrayal of Hassan and keeps that secret. Finally, when he knows himself to be nearing death, he takes the initiative in setting Amir on the road to redemption.

Hassan's family:

Ali - Ali is Baba's loyal, hard-working servant. He is content with his situation in life despite his poverty and the fact that, as a result of polio, he suffers from partial paralysis of his face and walks with a limp. This makes him the target of mockery by the local boys. Although it is never made totally clear in the novel, he must be aware that Hassan is the son of Baba by his former wife (Sanaubar). Nevertheless, he loves the boy deeply, though it is not his way openly to show his feelings.

Sanaubar - Hassan's mother deserts her husband Ali as soon as she has recovered from giving birth. She had a reputation for being immoral in her youth. However, when she returns as an old woman with scars across her face, she proves to be a caring grandmother to Hassan's son Sohrab until her death.

Hassan - Amir's best friend is raised as the son of Ali, a servant of Baba's. Father and son live alone because Hassan's mother abandoned them both shortly after Hassan was born. As the son of a poor ethnic Hazara and Sunni Muslim, Hassan is considered an inferior member of Afghan society, even by Amir who never regards him as his equal. Without education, Hassan is illiterate as a child (though as an adult he teaches himself to read), and Amir reads to him and invents stories to tell him.

Unknown to either boy, Hassan is actually Baba's illegitimate child, which explains Baba's occasional acts of generosity toward him. Although Hassan has always proved himself to be a loyal, brave and true friend to Amir, when Hassan needs his protection from three bullies, Amir lets him down. Amazingly, Hassan never holds this against his friend. Hassan's rape, and Amir's cowardly failure to prevent it initiates much of the plot of the novel.

Farzana - Hassan's wife and the mother of Sohrab is portrayed as a loving wife and mother. She reveres Hassan for his goodness.

Sohrab - Hassan and Farzana's son is a delightful child. His story is very like that of Hassan: his mother and father are murdered; he is persecuted for his ethnicity and religion; he is raped by the same man who violated Hassan. As a result, he becomes a traumatized victim of sexual and physical abuse. He attempts suicide, withdraws into himself, and refuses to speak. To what extent he will ever recover and be able to lead a 'normal' life is left unclear at the end.

Characters in Afghanistan:

Assef - The rapist both of Hassan and Sohrab, Assef is a sociopath and the novel's antagonist. He is not merely an individual but a living symbol of all the things that are wrong with Afghanistan: he is a racist prejudiced against Hazaras; he is a religious bigot prejudiced against Sunnis; he is a religious hypocrite who simply uses fundamentalist Islam for his own ends; and as a person he enjoys the sense of power he gets from inflicting violence and sexual abuse on the powerless. He never shows the slightest remorse for his cruelties.

Kamal and **Wali** - In the neighborhood of Kabul in which Amir lives, these two boys hang around with Assef who is very much the leader: they do what he says. Neither is willing to rape Hassan, but they do hold his arms while Assef violates him. Ironically, Kamal is later raped himself, so that he is both an embodiment of and a victim of the brutality that pervades Afghanistan.

Farid - Amir's driver upon his return to Pakistan and Afghanistan is originally antagonistic toward him, but when Farid learns the truth about Amir's reasons for his return he becomes his friend and loyal protector. Farid is a former mujahedin fighter, but he is now a bitter opponent of the forces that have brought so much suffering to Afghanistan. He is missing toes and fingers from a landmine explosion and struggling to earn enough to feed his family.

The Kite Runner by Khaled Hosseini

Characters in California:

General Taheri - Soraya's father and a friend of Baba, General Taheri, has been living in the Afghan community in San Francisco for several years by the time Baba and Amir get there. He is a traditionalist who places great value on upholding Afghan cultural and moral values. As a result, he perpetuates the inequality of women within his family, and considers working for a living to be beneath him. When Amir returns home with Sohrab, he is concerned for the reputation of the family now that Amir has introduced into it a Sunni Hazara. There are some signs however, that he is beginning to bend a little under the influence of American culture. Ultimately, he returns to Afghanistan to take up a government post.

Jamila - The General's wife and mother of Soraya is in many ways a typical Afghan wife and mother who obeys her husband and knows how important it is that her daughter is married. However, a closer look shows her to be a strong-willed woman who is not afraid to assert her opinion even when it contradicts that of her husband.

Sharif - Soraya's uncle attends her wedding. Later, he is able to use his influence and knowledge to help Amir bring Sohrab into the United States.

A Study Guide

Themes

Guilt / The Shadow of the Past

As we read on the first page, the past can never be buried. Afghanistan is to a large extent defined by its past. Since the time of Alexander the Great, the country has been invaded and fought over. Its present divisions whether ethnic, religious or sectarian) are the result of history.

On a personal level, each of the main characters feels the influence of decisions they have made in the past. It all begins with Baba's illicit sex with Sanaubar, and his failure to recognize the resulting baby as his son. Hosseini weaves a chain of causality from this 'original sin' right up to the death of Hassan at the hands of the Taliban and on to the trauma suffered by Sohrab.

Atonement / Redemption

Amir initially feels guilty because his mother died giving birth to him. In his eyes, this is why Baba does not show him the affection he desperately craves. (The real reason, of course, is Baba's own guilt over Hassan; he feels that he cannot show his true love for Amir because he cannot do the same for Hassan.) Amir believes that if he can win the kite-fighting tournament and bring Baba the losing kite, he will in some way atone for his mother's death and win his father's unreserved love. It is his single-minded pursuit of this goal that puts Hassan in a dangerous position, and it is his cowardice that prevents him from saving his friend from being raped. As a result, Amir feels an even greater sense of personal guilt, and it comes close to destroying him. However, many years later, his old mentor and surrogate father, Rahim Khan, offers him a way to redeem himself by returning to Afghanistan and rescuing Hassan's son Sohrab from the same fate that befell Hassan. To do this, Amir must be prepared to put his life in danger, that is, he must learn to have the courage of his convictions. Ironically, it was Baba who taught him this moral lesson, but it was Baba who first let Hassan down by not openly recognizing the boy as his son. What Amir achieves at the end can never put right the wrongs that have been done to the dead Hassan, and indeed may perhaps never put right the wrongs done to Sohrab, but the boy is given a chance: Amir has redeemed himself.

Family Relationships

Hosseini has said of his first two novels, "Characters seek and are saved by love and human connection. In *The Kite Runner*, it was mainly the love between men" (Book Browse Interview).

In Afghanistan relationships are constrained by cultural tradition. Those between husbands and wives are defined by traditional Islamic values which put all of the power in the hands of husbands. Similarly, relations between parents and children are culturally determined: males are valued above females and given greater freedom in their lives. In addition, every family jealously protects its honor and good name. For Baba to acknowledge paternity in the case of Hassan would be for him to lose his reputation. Girls are particularly vulnerable to gossip about their behavior; one example of misconduct (real or imagined) can make a young woman unmarriageable. In proposing to Soraya, Amir is able to overlook her youthful indiscretions, which no man in Afghanistan would be able to do. Mothers in the novel show unconditional love for their children whatever their gender, but fathers are more constrained. The most loving relationship between father and son is that of Hassan and Sohrab. Ironically, the one family relationship which is free from these constraints, and therefore ideal for children, is the childless union between Amir and Soraya. Amir tries to become a substitute father to Sohrab by applying the lessons in fatherhood that he has learned from Rahim Khan and from Hassan.

The Intersection of Political Events and Private Lives

As in Hosseini's second novel *A Thousand Splendid Suns*, the private lives and personal struggles of the main characters are played out in the context of political and military events which change the enlightened Kabul of Amir's childhood into a city ruled by Shari'a Law which is ruthlessly and publicly enforced. The eventual establishment of control over the city by the Taliban gives Assef an official position that allows him unrestrainedly to indulge his sadism and deviant sexual urges without any fear of being punished. In confronting Assef and saving Sohrab, Amir is symbolically making a personal stand against the ideology which has corrupted the interpretation of Islam to which he adheres.

Man's Capacity to Inflict Pain on Man

The war which appears to be endemic in Afghanistan has many victims. What the Taliban come to power the deliberate, calculated infliction of pain is raised to new levels. The description of the weekly punishments in the soccer stadium, and of the enthusiastic reaction of the crowd, is chilling.

Rape stands as a symbol for the physical and mental violation of the individual. The number of rapes in the novel is surprising: Assef's rape of Hassan, the soldier who wishes to trade the rape of woman for allowing the truck to proceed, the rape of Kamal, Assef's repeated rape of Sohrab. These acts take away from the victims their sense of self-worth and frequently leave them emotionally traumatized.

Two Ways of Representing the Narrative in Graphic Form

Readers will find a timeline and a family tree each of which will help them to understand the relationships between the characters and the historical context in which the personal lives of the characters play out.

Timeline: Although it happened long before the start of the novel, the relevant history of Afghanistan begins with the bloodless coup against King Zahir Shah who had ruled for forty years.

NOTE A timeline is included towards the end of the book for reference.

Family Tree: The lives of all of the main characters go back to the two boys fathered by Baba.- diagram provided towards the end of the book for reference.

Note for teachers

Since it would be too much to ask each student to produce both a timeline and a family tree, these could be group or class projects presented on charts and posted in the classroom for easy reference.

Students can note historic events on one side of the timeline and personal events on the other, using color coding and perhaps photographs

The Kite Runner by Khaled Hosseini

Study Guide

This novel deserves to be read *reflectively*. The questions are *not* designed to test you but to help you to locate and to understand characters, plot, settings, issues, and themes in the text. They do not normally have simple answers, nor is there always one answer. Consider a range of possible interpretations - preferably by *discussing* the questions with others. Disagreement is to be encouraged!

[Terms underlined in the text are explained in the "Glossary" that follows the questions.]

ONE: December 2001

The first-person narrator is Amir (38 years old), a native of Afghanistan who now lives in San Francisco. He begins with the statement that an incident that occurred in the winter of 1975 in Kabul, Afghanistan, made him "what I am today" (1). He does not say what the incident was (except that it was connected with looking into a deserted alley), but the reader notes that he uses the word "what" rather than "who." A letter from Rahim Khan in Pakistan and the sight of two kites reminds Amir of the two people who were an essential part of his childhood: Baba, his father, and Hassan, his best friend.

1. Other than those mentioned above, what other clue(s) do you find to the nature of the life-defining incident to which Amir refers?

TWO

The political and religious divisions in Afghanistan are very complex, so some explanation is required. Ali and his son Hassan are Hazaras; Amir and Baba are Pashtuns. The Hazara, who are Shi'a Muslims, have been for centuries systematically persecuted by the Pashtuns, who are Sunni Muslims.

2. What additional reasons are given for the low regard in which the Hazaras are held by Pashtuns?

THREE

This chapter explores the uneasy relationship that Amir and his father had, for whilst Amir admired his father tremendously, he was nothing like him in his interests and aptitudes. Amir once overheard his father telling his friend Rahim Khan, "'If I hadn't seen the doctor pull him out of my wife … I'd never believe he's my son'" (20). Amir carries the guilt of knowing that his beautiful mother died giving birth to him: he feels as though he killed her.

3. Explain the different religious perspectives of Amir's teacher, Mullah Fatiullah Khan, and his father Baba.

FOUR

Hassan is Amir's friend, but because of the social, ethnic and religious gulf between them Amir never refers to Hassan as his friend.

4. Comment on the significance of the adjective "somewhat" in the phrase describing the two men who killed the five-year-old boy (21).

5. Upon several occasions, Amir acts or thinks in mean, even cruel, ways towards Hassan. Give examples and explain Amir's <u>motivation</u>.

FIVE

The start of the chapter is a harsh reminder that the childhoods of Amir and Hassan (and the lives of all of the other characters) can be determined by factors entirely beyond their control or even their comprehension.

It is Hassan who saves Amir from a savage beating by the sociopathic Assef. It is becoming very clear that Amir feels a tremendous burden of guilt about Hassan. Presumably this explains the life-defining incident to which Amir refers in the first chapter.

6. How does Amir react to the birthday present that Baba gives to Hassan? How do you react to it?

SIX

Hassan "was by far the greatest kite runner" in Kabul because "he always got to the spot the kite would land before the kite did" as though by instinct (46). The reader notes that the novel is Hassan's story. The tragic story of the kite runner who broke his back falling from a tree seems like <u>foreshadowing</u>.

7. Why is it desperately important to Amir that he should win the kite fighting contest?

SEVEN

This chapter finally reveals the terrible incident. Amir reflects, "I opened my mouth, almost said something. Almost. The rest of my life might have turned out differently if I had" (64). Notice that the <u>narrator</u>'s focus is still on himself as victim. The real victim, however, is Hassan and what happens to him becomes a <u>symbol</u> for what happens to all of the poor and to the religious minorities (the two are virtually the same) in Afghanistan.

8. The description of what happens to Hassan is interrupted by two memories and a dream. Explain how each is related to what Amir sees and does (or does not do).

9. Amir writes, "Maybe Hassan was the price I had to pay … to win Baba" (68). Explain what he means by this.

EIGHT

Given that Amir's failure to protect Hassan was largely a result of his desire to win his father's approval, it is <u>ironic</u> that the guilt that he feels causes him to act in ways that further alienate the two. Firstly, Amir hints at changing the servants which angers and shames Baba, and secondly, he appears to be rude when accepting Assef's gift. Of course, the source of the problem is that Amir fears that he will irrevocably lose his father's love if he tells him what he actually did, or failed to do. (There is an even more fundamental <u>irony</u>. Amir's cowardice toward Hassan parallels Baba's cowardice toward Hassan by repeatedly failing to acknowledge him as his son.)

10. Explain what Amir means when he writes, "I understood the nature of my new curse: I was going to get away with it" (75).

11. Why does Rahim Khan tell Amir the story of his failed romance with Homaira? Explain what he is trying to tell Amir when he says, "'In the end, the world always wins. That's just the way of things'" (86).

12. What is the last thing that Amir sees in this chapter? What effect does it have on him?

NINE

The lie that Amir tells about Hassan stealing from him results in his discovery that not only does Hassan know that Amir watched him being raped and did nothing, but that he has told his father Ali what happened. When Hassan admits to the theft that he did not commit, Amir understands, "This was Hassan's final sacrifice for me" (91).

13. Explain fully why Baba forgives Hassan for the theft of Amir's presents to which he has admitted.

TEN: March 1981

During the Russian occupation of Afghanistan, Baba and Amir (now 18) are smuggled out of the country. They are forced to leave virtually everything they own behind. First, they are taken to Jalalabad and then, after a significant delay, into Peshawar in Pakistan. Two incidents reference the rape of Hassan that Amir witnessed and did nothing to stop. Firstly, a Russian checkpoint guard threatens to rape a young woman who is part of the group being smuggled. When no one else does so, Baba stands up to the soldier saying, "'Tell him I'll take a thousand bullets of his before I let this indecency take place'" (101). Baba's courage saves the young woman, and Amir is left to reflect on how differently he had acted. Secondly, Amir meets Kamal, one of the boys who held Hassan while he was raped. Ironically, Kamal is suffering from the trauma of having himself been raped: he cannot speak and his whole body is "withered" (104). Kamal dies, and his father commits suicide in front of Amir.

14. Contrast the views of the Russian guard and Baba on the place of decency during times of war.
15. Why does Baba become so furious with Karim when he discovers that the engine of the truck they need to take them out of the country blew up a week earlier?

ELEVEN

Baba and Amir react very differently to living in America. Partly, this is simply a matter of age - Baba is around fifty. However, Baba is an idealist and still holds to the values that epitomized Afghan society at its best: self-reliance, honor, trust, and honesty. These are values he does not find in America.

16. Why does Baba react so violently when the Vietnamese shop owner asks him to show his ID?
17. Amir uses the following <u>metaphor</u> to describe living in the U.S.A., "America was a river, roaring along, unmindful of the past" (119). Explain fully what you think that he means by this metaphor.
18. What similarities do you find between the pasts of Amir and of Soraya Teheri?

TWELVE

Two plot developments occur: Baba's declining health and Amir's courtship of Soraya Teheri. Amir runs up against Afghan culture and values in the way that he approaches Soraya. Like a Westerner, he clearly wants to get to know her before he proposes, but this is not the way in which General Taheri, who "'is a Pashtun to the root'" (126), does things.

19. Why does General Taheri take the copies of Amir's story that he has given to Soraya and drop "the rolled pages into the garbage can" (133)?
20. What is illogical about Baba's reaction to Dr. Schneider? Why does Baba reject Amir's attempt to defend the doctor's heritage?
21. What similarities, and what differences, are there between the mistake that Soraya made in her life and Amir's error? In your opinion, should Amir have shared the truth of his cowardice with Soraya? Does Amir himself feel that he should have done so?

THIRTEEN

This chapter turns a much more critical light on Afghan culture. Amir, who is rapidly becoming American is deeply conscious of the double standard that exists in the way Afghan society treats men and women regarding sex. His wife, Soraya, complains that, while she was no longer considered virtuous after she ran away with a man, males are allowed to experiment sexually without facing condemnation.

22. The General represents the best and the worst aspects of Afghan culture. What details are given of his unequal treatment of women, particularly his own wife? What other negative aspects of his life are revealed?
23. Speaking of his and his wife's failure to have children, Amir says, "Maybe this was my punishment, and perhaps justly so" (164). Do you think that Amir will ever lay the ghost of his guilt? How might he do this?
24. Comment on Amir's use of this <u>simile</u>, "I could almost feel the emptiness in Soraya's womb, like it was a living, breathing thing ... I'd feel it rising from Soraya and settling between us. Seeping between us. Like a newborn child" (165).

FOURTEEN: June 2001 & FIFTEEN

The telephone call Amir gets from Rahim Khan is the call he refers to in Chapter One. After ten years of marriage, Amir and (he senses) Soraya feel that their love making is "futile" because both have given up hope of her conceiving. He continues to associate the barrenness of his marriage with his personal sense of guilt over Hassan.
Amir arrives in Peshawar to visit the ailing Rahim Khan with whom he

has lost touch for so many years. From him Amir hears first-hand about the victory of the Northern Alliance over the Russians, the oppression during its occupation of Kabul, and of the joy when the Taliban kicked them out. In the next chapter, he will relate the subsequent oppression of the people by the Taliban.

24. Rahim tells Amir, "*Come. There is a way to be good again ...*" (168). What does Amir assume that Rahim means by this?
25. What exactly is meant by the cliché "elephant in the room" (172)? When Amir sits down to talk to Rahim, there are several 'elephants in the room.' What are they?

SIXTEEN
Amir learns that in 1986 Rahim travelled to Hazarajat, found Hassan and brought him and his wife (Farzana) back to live at Baba's Kabul house and help with its up-keep. He learns that Hassan's first child was still-born, that his mother (Sanaubar) returned to him, that his second child (a boy called Sohrab) was born healthy, and that his mother died four years later. In 1996, the Taliban took over and the massacring of ethnic Hazaras began.

25. The story of Hassan's life seems to be one of unremitting hardship and tragedy. One wonders how he survives it. There have been several portraits in the narrative of less than perfect father-

son relationships. How does Hassan measure up as a father?

SEVENTEEN
This is a chapter of revelations which, for Amir, are shocking. First, he learns of the murder of Hassan and Farzana by members of the Taliban, and then that their son, Sohrab, is in an orphanage in Kabul. Second, he learns that Rahim wants him (Amir) to go to Kabul and rescue Sohrab. This is obviously the action that Rahim believes to be the way for Amir "*to be good again*" (2, 168). Since I can't put it any better, I will quote from SparkNotes, "By rescuing Sohrab, Amir can become the man that Baba always wanted him to be, and he can finally atone for the ways he failed Hassan as a friend."
Notice that in his letter to Amir, Hassan writes, "every day I thank Allah that I am alive, not because I fear death, but because my wife has a husband and my son is not an orphan" (190). That wish will prove to be

incredibly powerful in Amir's mind.

26. What relationship does Amir discover to exist between himself and Sohrab? (Probably the best way to understand what Rahim tells Amir at the end of this chapter is to produce a family tree. What Rahim tells Amir makes perfect sense to him but the reader struggles to understand its implications. The author *wants* the reader to struggle to understand its implications.)

EIGHTEEN

27. In what ways does Amir now realize that he is more like his father than he ever suspected?

NINETEEN

The journey over the Khyber Pass with Farid is physically and emotionally uncomfortable for Amir. Farid jumps to lots of conclusions about Amir - all of them negative. Farid's attitude to his passenger, however, changes when Amir reveals to Farid's brother, Wahid, the true reason for his journey to Kabul.

28. What does Farid get right about Amir's Afghan background?
29. Comment on Amir's feelings about his own writing when Wahid asks, "'Do you write about Afghanistan?'" (206).
30. Explain the nightmare that Amir has.
31. What is the first act of atonement for his sins against Hassan?

TWENTY

"Farid had warned me. He had. But as it turned out he had wasted his breath" (213). Nothing could have prepared Amir for the reality of the terrible changes in Kabul after two decades of warfare and tyrannical government. In enforcing their particular interpretation of the Koran (Shari'a Law), the Taliban ensure that all men grow their beards and prevent women from working: actually, many of the men have been killed in the fighting leaving the women to bring up the children, which they cannot do because they are not allowed to work. Society is literally crumbling.

By pure chance, Amir meets an old man who knew his mother when both he and she were teachers at the university. The orphanage, and particularly the way in which the unpaid director finances the institution, are a shock to every moral value Amir holds.

17

32. Why does the director accept money from the Talib official who comes once every month or two?

TWENTY-ONE

Amir finds the pomegranate tree into which he and Hassan used to climb, but it no longer bears fruit: the barren tree is a <u>symbol</u> of what Kabul has become.

The description of the stoning to death in the soccer stadium is horrific, although the author avoids going into graphic detail. It is particularly so because of the evident hypocrisy of those in charge: the Muslim cleric who gives the sermon is described as "chubby" and "plump" (235, 238), making it clear that the Taliban get plenty to eat; and the tall Talib who is in charge of the punishment of two adulterers, the man who actually throws the stones that batter each to death, is the same pedophile who takes children from the orphanage.

33. Jokes are never funny when they are explained, but the two mullah jokes (232-3) need to be explained. How does each mock the ignorance of the mullahs?

34. What precisely prompts Amir to reflect, "maybe what people said about Afghanistan was true. Maybe it *was* hopeless place" (233)?

35. What is particularly ironic about the Taliban official being repeatedly compared with John Lennon? (For those not familiar with this member of *The Beatles*, research is in order!)

TWENTY-TWO

Amir's confrontation with the Taliban official is initially tense and ultimately brutal. The Tamil boasts of having been involved in the massacre of Hazaras in Mazar-i-Sharif. He seems to glory in violence for its own sake.

Coincidence often plays an important role in novels. We have already noticed that Amir happens to talk to an old man in Kabul who knew his mother. However, Kabul is not a huge city and Afghans tend to live in distinct neighborhoods where the ties of family and friendship are strong. That the man turns out to be Assef is not so very unlikely. Assef is a survivor: he will adapt to any regime that he needs to in order to stay alive and to retain power over others. This time, however, Amir does not back down: he atones for his cowardly abandonment of Hassan by not abandoning his son who is also being raped by Assef. Sohrab saves Amir by hitting Assef in the left eye with his slingshot, thus performing the action that his father, Hassan, had threatened but never done.

36. Explain how Assef came to be a highly placed and powerful Taliban official

37. As he is being beaten by Assef, Amir thinks "for the first time since the winter of 1975, I felt at peace. I laughed because I saw that, in some hidden nook in a corner of my mind, I'd even been looking forward to this" (252). Explain Amir's reaction.

TWENTY-THREE
Amir's injuries are severe, but he clearly gets the very best medical care at the hospital in Peshawar. His upper lip has been sliced open and has required stitches: he will have a scar like Hassan's for the rest of his life.

In his letter to Amir, Rahim Khan admits that Baba did many things that were wrong, but he argues that in attempting to atone for his sins Baba also did a great deal of good, like building the orphanage. Life, it emerges, is complex!

38. How does Amir react when he hears about his cut lip and the prediction of the plastic surgeons that he will be left with a scar? Do you find the writer's use of <u>symbolism</u> at this point convincing and effective?

39. Amir has a dream in which Assef tells him, "'We're the same, you and I. You nursed with him, but you're *my* twin'" (268). In what ways are the two (at least up to this point) similar?

40. Farid tells Amir, "'There never was a John and Betty Caldwell in Peshawar … they never existed'" (269). Can you explain this? [Clue: In the last two sentences of this chapter, Amir understands it.]

TWENTY-FOUR
Omar Faisal, an immigration attorney tells Amir that his best chance of getting Sohrab to the States is to place him in an orphanage in Pakistan, file a petition, and wait up to two years for the government to approve the adoption. Amir has given Sohrab his word that he will never have to go back to an orphanage, but (in the face of reality) he has to go back on his word.

The reader will notice that from the time he left the hospital little has been said about Amir's injuries. The timeline is a little fuzzy at this part in the narrative (understandable given the narrator's physical and emotional state), but nevertheless he appears to have recovered enough to move around and see people rather quickly. Similarly, given the advice that Amir is given by Raymond Andrews at the American Embassy and by Omar Faisal, two men who must know the laws on immigration inside-out, it is perhaps surprising that Soraya, after a few phone calls, learns that they can quickly get Sohrab into the States on a humanitarian visa and once there "'there are ways of keeping him here'" (298). Both Amir's recovery and the solution to Sohrab's immigration problem *may* seem to the reader to be a little too convenient.

41. The chapter ends with a tremendous 'hook' (i.e., a sentence that makes the reader desperate to read on. What do you think has happened?

TWENTY-FIVE

General Taheri represents traditional Afghanistan, in both its positive and its negative aspects. Concerned about his family's reputation, he asks why Amir brought a Hazara boy into the family. This is in many ways Amir's biggest challenge in the book. He must sweep away the hypocrisy which was at the foundation of Afghan society and begin to establish a new Afghan culture based on honesty and equality for all sects and classes: he passes the test effortlessly by standing up to his father-in-law. Amir says that his Baba slept with a servant woman and that Sohrab is the son of their child, his own half-brother Hassan's which makes Sohrab Amir's nephew: finally the truth is out there. Firmly, Amir tells General Taheri never to call Sohrab a "Hazara boy" in his presence again but to use the boy's name.

The novel ends with Amir going to run the kite whose string he has cut for Sohrab. Amir says to Sohrab the last words Hassan said to him before Hassan was raped. In this sense the ending is highly symbolic and perhaps a little too contrived. In other ways, the novel ends with many issues unresolved, and with no guarantee of a 'happily ever after' future.

42. What issues are unresolved at the end of the novel?

The Kite Runner by Khaled Hosseini

Glossary of literary terms (useful in discussing this novel)

first-person narrator/narrative - The narrative in a work of fiction may either be third or first person. Third person narrative is told by an unidentified voice which belongs to someone not directly involved in the events narrated. First person narrative means that story is told from the necessarily limited viewpoint of one of the characters writing or speaking directly about themselves and their experience.

foreshadowing - An author uses foreshadowing when he/she hints at a future development in the plot. This builds up the reader's involvement in the fiction.

image - Imagery is a blanket term that describes the use of figurative language to represent objects, actions and ideas in such a way that it appeals to our five physical senses. Thus, amongst others, similes, metaphors and symbolism are examples of images.

> *metaphor* - A metaphor is a implied comparison in which whatever is being described is referred to as though it were another thing (e.g., "To be, or not to be: that is the question: / Whether 'tis nobler in the mind to suffer / The *slings and arrows* of outrageous *fortune*, / Or to take arms against *a sea of troubles*, / And by opposing end them?" Shakespeare *Hamlet*)

> *simile* - A simile is a descriptive comparison which uses the words "like" or "as" to make the intended comparison clear (e.g., "O my Luve's like a red, red rose / That's newly sprung in June; / O my Luve's like the melodie / That's sweetly play'd in tune." Robert Burns).

> *symbol* - A description in which one thing stand for or represents or suggests something bigger and more significant than itself. Normally a material object is used to represent an idea, belief, action, theme, person, etc. (e.g., in the Burns poem above, he uses the rose because it is a traditional symbol for love, passion, emotion and romance just as the sun became a natural and almost universal symbol of kingship).

irony / ironic - The essential feature of irony is the presence of a contradiction between an action or expression and the meaning it has in the context in which it occurs. Writers are always conscious of using irony, but there characters may either be aware or unaware that something that they say or do is ironic. Dramatic irony is the term used to describe a character saying or doing something that has significance for the audience or reader but of which the characters are not aware. For example, when

Othello says, "If it were now to die, / 'Twere now to be most happy, for I fear /
My soul hath her content so absolute / That not another comfort like to this / Succeeds in unknown fate" (*Othello* 2:1), this is dramatic irony because the audience knows that he speaks truer than he knows.

motivation - Since Sigmund Freud 'invented' psychoanalysis, motivation has predominantly been though or in terms of psychology. Thus, the actions of a character may surprise us but they should also strike us as psychologically plausible.

Further Reading

A Thousand Splendid Suns, Hosseini's second novel is even better than his first. It tells the story of two women born in Afghanistan in the second half of the twentieth century. Mariam, born in Heart in the 1960s, is the illegitimate daughter of a wealthy businessman who refuses to recognize her as part of his family and is brought up by her embittered mother; Laila, born in Kabul in the 1970s, is the daughter of intellectual parents who teach her the value of education and inspire her to want to make a contribution to improving society. Circumstances bring these two different women together as the wives of Rasheed, a shoemaker in Kabul.

The Kite Runner by Khaled Hosseini

Using the Study Guide Questions

Although there are both closed and open questions in the Study Guide, very few of them have simple, right or wrong answers. They are designed to encourage in-depth discussion, disagreement, and (eventually) consensus. Above all, they aim to encourage students to go to the text to support their conclusions and interpretations.

I am not so arrogant as to presume to tell teachers how they should use this resource. I used it in the following ways, each of which ensured that students were well prepared for class discussion and presentations.

1. Set a reading assignment for the class and tell everyone to be aware that the questions will be the focus of whole class discussion the next class.

2. Set a reading assignment for the class and allocate particular questions to sections of the class (e.g. if there are four questions, divide the class into four sections, etc.).

In class, form discussion groups containing one person who has prepared each question and allow time for feedback within the groups.

Have feedback to the whole class on each question by picking a group at random to present their answers and to follow up with class discussion.

3. Set a reading assignment for the class, but do not allocate questions.

In class, divide students into groups and allocate to each group one of the questions related to the reading assignment the answer to which they will have to present formally to the class.

Allow time for discussion and preparation.

4. Set a reading assignment for the class, but do not allocate questions.

In class, divide students into groups and allocate to each group one of the questions related to the reading assignment.

Allow time for discussion and preparation.

Now reconfigure the groups so that each group contains at least one person who has prepared each question and allow time for feedback within the groups.

5. Before starting to read the text, allocate specific questions to individuals or pairs. (It is best not to allocate all questions to allow for other approaches and variety. One in three questions or one in four seems about right.) Tell students that they will be leading the class discussion on their question. They will need to start with a brief presentation of the issues and then conduct a question and answer session. After this, they will be expected to present a brief review of the discussion.

6. Having finished the text, arrange the class into groups of 3, 4 or 5. Tell each group to select as many questions from the Study Guide as there are members of the group.

Each individual is responsible for drafting out a written answer to one question, and each answer should be a substantial paragraph.

Each group as a whole is then responsible for discussing, editing and suggesting improvements to each answer, which is revised by the original writer and brought back to the group for a final proof reading followed by revision.

This seems to work best when the group knows that at least some of the points for the activity will be based on the quality of all of the answers.

The Kite Runner by Khaled Hosseini

Graphic organizer: Plot

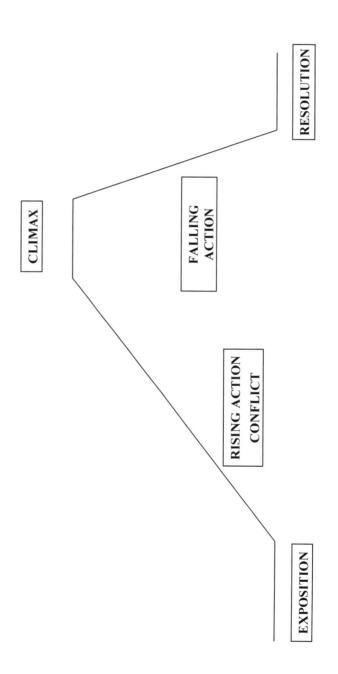

Plot graph for *The Kite Runner*

CLIMAX

RESOLUTION

FALLING ACTION

RISING ACTION CONFLICT

EXPOSITION

Graphic organizer: Perspectives

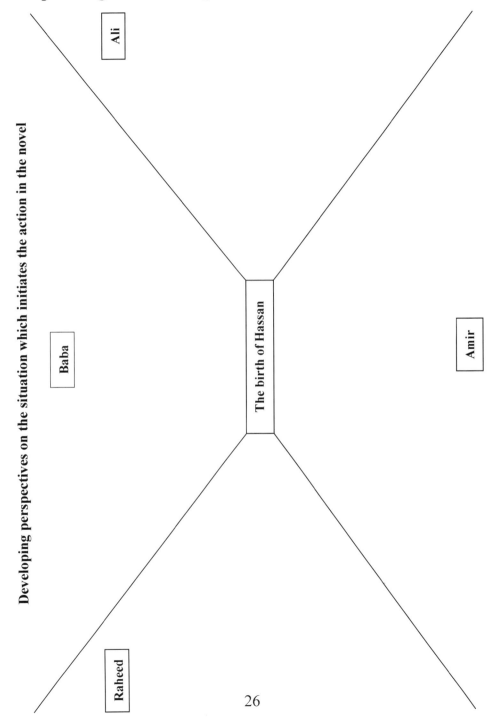

Developing perspectives on the situation which initiates the action in the novel

Ali

Baba

Raheed

The birth of Hassan

Amir

The Kite Runner by Khaled Hosseini

FamilyTree

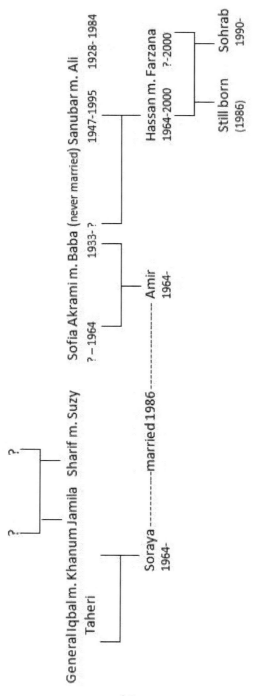

Timeline

Afghanistan's history	Dates		Events in the book
		1928	**Ch. 4** Ali is born.
		1933	**Ch. 4** Baba is born
		1963	**Ch. 3** Amir is born, but his mother dies.
		1964	**Ch. 2** Hassan is born. Events from Amir and Hassan's childhood are related. Ali had polio resulting in an atrophied right leg (limps, peculiar gait)
		1968 - 1971	**Ch. 3** Baba builds an orphanage. Baba and his friend Rahim Khan create a successful carpet-exporting business, 2 pharmacies and a restaurant. Amir hates sports. loves to read.
Mohammed Daoud Khan declares himself President in a coup against the king, Mohammed Zahir Shah.	17 July	1973	**Ch. 4** Amir reads to Hassan and starts to create stories of his own. Rahim encourages him to write. **Ch. 5** Amir and Hassan are threatened by Assef, Wali and Kamal. Hassan defends them with his slingshot.

			Ch. 5 contd. Life in Kabul is described. Baba arranges for a plastic surgeon to operate on Hassan's cleft lip.
		1975	**Ch. 6** Kite fighting and kite running explained. Amir is a kite fighter, Hassan is the kite runner. **Ch. 7** Amir wins the kite competition. Hassan runs and gets the last kite. The incident referred to in **Ch. 1** occurs. Amir sees it but runs away. **Ch. 8** Baba, Amir and family visit Jalalabad. Amir pulls away from Hassan.
		1976	**Ch. 8** Amir's 13th birthday. Ramir gives him a notebook. **Ch. 9** His father gives him a bike and a wristwatch. Amir says he has lost the watch, but hides it under Hassan's mattress. Hassan confesses to stealing but is innocent. Ali and Hassan leave.
Saur Revolution: Military units loyal to the PDPA assaulted the Afghan Presidential	27 April	1978	

Palace, killing President Mohammed Daoud Khan and his family.			
The PDPA installed its leader, Nur Muhammad Taraki, as President of Afghanistan.	1 May		
A rebellion against the new Afghan government began with an uprising in Nuristan Province.	July		
A treaty was signed which permitted deployment of the Soviet military at the Afghan government's request.	5 December		
Taraki was murdered by supporters of Prime Minister Hafizullah Amin.	14 September		
Soviet intervention (1979-1989)		1979	
Soviet war in Afghanistan: Fearing the collapse of the Amin regime, the Soviet army invaded Afghanistan.	24 December		
Operation Storm-333: Soviet troops occupied major governmental, military and media	27 December		

buildings in Kabul, including the Tajbeg Palace, and executed Prime Minister Amin.			
		1981	**Ch. 10** Baba and Amir are smuggled out of Afghanistan and into Pakistan. They travel on to America after getting visas. **Ch. 15** Rahim moves into Baba's house.
		1983	**Ch. 11** Amir attends High School, graduating in 1983. Baba gives Amir a car the day he graduates.
		1984	**Ch. 11** Baba makes money selling at the San Jose flea market. They meet General Taheri there, who also has a stand with his family.
		1985	**Ch. 12** Amir gets to know Soraya Taheri. Baba is ill.
		1986	**Ch. 12** Baba arranges Amir's marriage to Soraya. **Ch. 13** Amir and Soraya marry. Baba dies a month later. The General gives Amir a typewriter. Amir enrolls at san jose State College

			Ch. 16 Rahim finds Hassan and his wife and takes them back to Baba's house in Kabul. Hassan has learned to read and write. Farzana's child is still born.
		1987	**Ch. 13** Soraya enrolls in a teaching course at San Jose State
The Soviet government signed the Geneva Accords, which included a timetable for withdrawing their armed forces.	14 April	1988	**Ch. 13** Amir gets an agent and his first story is accepted for publication.
The last Soviet troops left the country.	15 February	1989	**Ch. 13** Amir's novel is released. They try unsuccessfully to have a baby.
		1990	**Ch. 16** Sanaubar returns to Baba's house. She helps deliver Farzana's son, Sohrab.
		1991	**Ch. 13** they consider adopting a child.
Civil war in Afghanistan (1989-1992): Afghan political parties signed the Peshawar Accord which created the Islamic State of Afghanistan and proclaimed	24 April	1992	**Ch. 15** Rahim relates how in 1992-1996 moving through the streets of Kabul is hazardous as the warlords control different areas.

Sibghatullah Mojaddedi its interim President.			
Gulbuddin Hekmatyar's Hezbi Islami, with the support of neighboring Pakistan, began a massive bombardment against the Islamic State in the capital Kabul.			
As agreed upon in the Peshawar Accord, Jamiat-e Islami leader Burhanuddin Rabbani took over as President.	28 June		
The Durand line Treaty is expired and all Afghans lands are supposed to be returned but Pakistan refuses to.	January	1993	
The Taliban government began to form in a small village between Lashkar Gah and Kandahar.	August	1994	
The Taliban, with Pakistani support, initiated a military campaign against the Islamic State of Afghanistan and its capital Kabul.	January	1995	**Ch. 14**. Amir and Soraya get a dog Aflatoon. **Ch 16.** Sanaubar dies.
The Taliban, tortured and killed Abdul Ali Mazari leader of the	13 March		

Hazara people.			
Civil war in Afghanistan (1996-2001): The forces of the Islamic State retreated to northern Afghanistan.	26 September		
The Taliban conquered Kabul and declared the establishment of the Islamic Emirate of Afghanistan. Former President Mohammad Najibullah, who had been living under United Nations protection in Kabul, was tortured, castrated and executed by Taliban forces.	27 September	1996	**Ch. 16** Hassan has taught his son to read and write and he teaches him kite running.
The Taliban captured Mazar-e Sharif, forcing Abdul Rashid Dostum into exile.	August	1998	**Ch. 16** Kite fighting is banned by the Taliban.
Cruise missile strikes on Afghanistan and Sudan: Cruise missiles were fired by the US Navy into 4 militant training camps in the Islamic Emirate of Afghanistan.	20 August	1998	
		1999	**Ch. 14** General Taheri breaks his hip.
		2000	**Ch. 17** Hassan and his

The Kite Runner by Khaled Hosseini

			wife are killed.
Resistance leader Ahmad Shah Massoud was killed in a suicide bomb attack by two Arabs who disguised as French news reporters.	9 September		**Ch. 1** Amir's story begins to be told. **Ch. 14** June- Rahim Khan is sick. Amir leaves California for Peshawar, Pakistan.
After the September 11 attacks in the United States, U.S. President George W. Bush demanded the Taliban government to hand over al-Qaeda head Osama bin Laden and close all terrorist training camps in the country.	20 September	2001	**Ch. 15** Memories of leaving in 1981. Amir tells Rahim about his life in America, **Ch. 17** Rahim asks Amir to rescue Sohrab and reveals that Hassan is Amir's half-brother. **Ch. 18** Amir reflects on the past in the light of this information.
The Taliban refused Bush's ultimatum for lack of evidence connecting bin Laden to 9/11 attacks.	21 September		**Ch. 19** Amir is driven to Kabul by Farid. he explains to Wahid, Farid's brother why he has come.
Operation Enduring Freedom: The United States and the United Kingdom began an aerial bombing campaign against al-Qaeda and the Taliban.	7 October		**Ch. 20** Amir visits the orphanage. Sohrab was taken by a Taliban soldier. **Ch 21** Amir goes to Ghazi Stadium to find the boy. Prisoners at stoned at half-time in the football match.
The United Nations Security Council authorized the creation of the International Security Assistance Force (ISAF) to help	5 December		**Ch. 22** The Taliban soldier is Assef! Amir and Hassan fight and Sohrab blinds Assef in

maintain security in Afghanistan and assist the Karzai administration			one eye with his slingshot. **Ch. 23** Farid takes Amir and Sohrab to Peshwar where Amir's life is saved at the hospital. Farid takes Amir and Sohrab to Islamabad. **Ch. 24** Amir asks Sohrab to come back to America with him. Sohrab agrees, but they need a visa for him. **Ch. 25** Sohrab tries to commit suicide when it seems that he would have to live in an orphanage before he can get a visa to leave. When he recovers they go to America.
International Conference on Afghanistan in Germany: Hamid Karzai chosen as head of the Afghan Interim Administration.	20 December		
2002 Loya jirga (general assembly in Kabul): Hamid Karzai appointed as President of the Afghan Transitional Administration in Kabul, Afghanistan.	July	2002	**Ch. 25** An Afghan celebration in the Bay area involves kite flying and Amir and Sohrab reconnect.
2003 A 502-delegate loya jirga was held to consider a new Afghan constitution.	14 December	2003	
Hamid Karzai was elected President of the Islamic Republic of	9 October	2004	

The Kite Runner by Khaled Hosseini

Afghanistan after winning the Afghan presidential election.			

The section of the timeline that deals with Afghan history is reproduced with slight revisions from the Wikipedia article "Timeline of Afghan history." (Reproduced on the basis of the Creative Commons License: http://creativecommons.org/licenses/by-sa/3.0/)

Arabic/ Persian Glossary

Ahesta boro: wedding song

Ahmaq: foolish, stupid, awkward

Al hamdullellah: "Thanks to God."

Alahoo: whilst swinging back and forth - a phrase/song said mostly for little kids

Allah-u-akbar: "Allah is the greatest." The phrase 'allahu akbar' is the opening declaration of every Islamic prayer

Alef-beh: the letters a (alef) and b (beh), used to signify the alphabet

Arg: place in Kabul

Attan: Pashtun tribal dance

Aush: soup

Awroussi: traditional Afghan wedding dance

Ayat: prayer

Ayats: verse of the Koran

Ayat-ul-kursi: Ayat al-kursi is verse 255 of the second chapter (surah) of the holy Koran.

Ayena masshaf: ceremony involving mirrors in order for the couple to gaze at each other's reflection.

Azan: call to prayer

Baba: father

Babalu: bogeyman

Bachem: "My son," or "My child."

Balay: "I do," or "Yes."

Baksheesh: forgiveness

Bakhshida: forgiven

Bas: enough

Bazarris: bazaar

Bia: come

Biryani: Indian dish of meat, vegetables and yogurt

Bismillah!: "In the name of God!"

Biwa: widow

Boboresh!: "Cut him!"

Bolani: vegan flat-bread, baked or fried with a vegetable filling

Burqa: head-to-toe covering worn by women

Buzkashi: The national sport played on horseback, involves capturing a goat or calf carcass and dropping it into a scoring circle.

Chai: tea

Chaman: the capital of Qilla Abdullah district, Baluchistan, Pakistan

Chapan: coat adorned with intricate threading worn over clothes, usually during the cold winter months and usually by men

Chapandaz: highly skilled Buzkashi player

Chila: wedding ring

Deh- mazang: district of Kabul

The Kite Runner by Khaled Hosseini

Dil: heart

Dil-roba: heart-thief

Dogh: yoghurt drink

Dostet darum: "I love you."

Eid: three days of celebration after the holy month of Ramadan

Eid mubarak: Happy Eid

Eid of qorban,: Muslim ceremony remembering Abraham's willingness to sacrifice his son

Ferni: sweet rice pudding

Ghamkori: self-pity

Ghazal: poetry form from Persia consisting of rhyming couplets and a refrain

Goshkhor: ear-eater

Gung bichara: expression of empathy

Hadia: gift

Haddith: collection of the reports purporting to quote what the Islamic prophet Muhammad said verbatim on any matter

Hadj (of haj, or hajj): pilgrimage to Mecca

Hazara: ethnic group of the Hazarajat region in central Afghanistan

Hijab: veil that covers the head and chest, which is often worn by Muslim women beyond the age of puberty in the presence of adult males

Iftchkhar: pride

Ihitiram: respect

Inshallah: "God willing."

Isfand: wild plant that is burned for its aroma and to ward off misfortune

Jadi: December

Jai-namaz: prayer rug

Jan: term of endearment

Jaroo: broomstick

Kaka: uncle

Kamyab: rare, unique

Kandahar: second largest city in Afghanistan

Kasseef: filthy

Khala: aunt (on the mother's side of the family)

Khanum: lady, wife

Kha khara mishnassah: "It takes a donkey to know a donkey."

Khastegar: suitor

Khastegari: suitor's official visit to the family to propose marriage

Kho dega: "So!"

Khoda lafez: until then

Khoshteep: handsome

Kocheh-morga: chicken bazaar

Kochi: nomad

Kofta: meatball

Kolcha: type of bread

Kursi: electric heater under a table usually covered with a thick quilt/ blanket

A Study Guide

La illaha il Allah, Muhammad u rasul ullah:
"There is no God but Allah and Muhammad is his messenger."

Laaf: exaggeration

Lafz: ceremony of betrothal

Lawla: tulip flowers

Lotfan: please

Maghbool: attractive

Madar: mother

Maghout: almond topped cookie

Mantu: sheep's stomach stuffed with rice

Mar: man, hero

Mashallah!: "Praise God!"

Masnawi: six volume poem by Rumi

Mast: drunk

Mehmanis: parties

Moalem: teacher

Moftakhir: proud

Mohtaram: respected

Mojarad: single man

Mord: dead

Morgh: chicken

Mozahem: intruder

Mujahedin: guerrilla military outfits led by Muslim afghan warriors in the soviet war in Afghanistan, but later fought each other.

Mueszzin: the person appointed at a mosque to lead, and recite, the call to prayer

Mullah: title of respect for a person learned in sacred law

Naan: flatbread

Nah-kam: unlucky

Namaz: prayers prescribed by law to be recited five times a day

Namoos: pride

Nang: honor

Naswar: smokeless chewing tobacco

Nawasi: grandchild

Nazr: a vow to give the meat of a slaughtered sheep to the poor.

Nihari: beef or lamb curry

Nika: swearing ceremony of a wedding

Pakeeza: 1972 Indian film

Pakol: a soft, rounded, afghan or Pashtun man's hat, usually wool and an earthy color

Pakora: a fried snack

Panjpar: a card game

Parchami: communist

Pari: angel

Pashtun: ethnic afghan

Pirhan-tumban: traditional shirt and pants

Qaom: family member

Qawali: sufi devotional music

Qiyamat: judgement day

Qorban, Eid of: Muslim ceremony remembering Abraham's willingness to sacrifice his son

Qurma: stew

The Kite Runner by Khaled Hosseini

Quwat: power, force

Rafiq: comrade

Raka't: section of prayer

Rawsti: anyway, after all

Rooussi: Russian

Rubab: four-stringed instrument, like a short-necked guitar but with a parchment surface in place of wood.

Rupia: unit of currency

Sabiz challow: white rice with spinach and lamb

Sahib: sir

Salaam: hello

Salaam alaykum: hello to you

Salaam bachem; hello my child

Samosa: triangular pastry stuffed with minced meat

Sawl-e-nau: Afghan New Year's Day

Seh-parcha: fabric

Shahbas!: bravo!

Shahnamah: tenth-century epic book of ancient Persian heroes

Shalwar-kameez: long shirt and pantaloons (wide pants)

Shari'a: the Islamic legal system derived from the religious precepts of Islam

Sherjangi: battle of the poems

Shi'a Muslim: a Muslim of the second-largest denomination of Islam

Shirini-khori: "eating of sweets" ceremony

Sholeh- goshti: a kind of food

Shorawi: Russians - then the USSR

Shorwa: simple soup eaten in Afghanistan

Sunni Muslim: a Muslim of the largest denomination of Islam

Surah: a chapter in the sacred scripture of Islam,

Tandoor: cooking oven

Tar: a glass coated cutting line for a kite

Tashakor: thank you

Tashweesh: nervousness

Toophan agha: Mr. Hurricane

Topeh chasht: cannons fired at noon or to signal the end of the daylight fasting during Ramadan

Tu: you (familiar address) *shoma:* you (formal address)

Wah wah: bravo admirable

Watan: homeland

Yelda: first night of winter and the longest night of the year

Ya Mowlah: a piece of music or a song

Zakat: a form of obligatory alms-giving and religious tax in Islam

Zendagi: life

zendagi migzara: Life goes on

(Note: The glossary has been compiled from a number of sources.)

41

A Study Guide

To the Reader
Ray strives to make his products the best that they can be. If you have any comments or questions about this book *please* contact the author through his email: **moore.ray1@yahoo.com**
Visit his website at **http://www.raymooreauthor.com**
Also by Ray Moore: Most books are available from amazon.com as paperbacks and at most online eBook retailers.

Fiction:
The Lyle Thorne Mysteries: each book features five tales from the Golden Age of Detection:
> *Investigations of The Reverend Lyle Thorne*
> *Further Investigations of The Reverend Lyle Thorne*
> *Early Investigations of Lyle Thorne*
> *Sanditon Investigations of The Reverend Lyle Thorne*
> *Final Investigations of The Reverend Lyle Thorne*

Non-fiction:
The ***Critical Introduction series*** is written for high school teachers and students and for college undergraduates. Each volume gives an in-depth analysis of a key text:
> *"The Stranger" by Albert Camus: A Critical Introduction* (Revised Second Edition)
> *"The General Prologue" by Geoffrey Chaucer: A Critical Introduction*
> *"Pride and Prejudice" by Jane Austen: A Critical Introduction*
> *"The Great Gatsby" by F. Scott Fitzgerald: A Critical Introduction*

The Text and Critical Introduction series <u>differs</u> from the Critical Introduction series as these books contain the original text and in the case of the medieval texts an interlinear translation to aid the understanding of the text. The commentary allows the reader to develop a deeper understanding of the text and themes within the text.
> *"Sir Gawain and the Green Knight": Text and Critical Introduction*
> *"The General Prologue" by Geoffrey Chaucer: Text and Critical Introduction*
> *"The Wife of Bath's Prologue and Tale" by Geoffrey Chaucer: Text and Critical Introduction*
> *"Heart of Darkness" by Joseph Conrad: Text and Critical Introduction*
> *"The Sign of Four" by Sir Arthur Conan Doyle Text and Critical Introduction*
> *A Room with a View"* By E.M. Forster: Text and Critical Introduction

The Kite Runner by Khaled Hosseini

Study guides available in print- listed alphabetically by author

* denotes also available as an eBook

"Wuthering Heights" by Emily Brontë: A Study Guide *

"Jane Eyre" by Charlotte Brontë: A Study Guide *

"The Meursault Investigation" by Kamel Daoud: A Study Guide

"Great Expectations" by Charles Dickens: A Study Guide *

"The Myth of Sisyphus" and "The Stranger" by Albert Camus: Two Study Guides *

"The Sign of Four" by Sir Arthur Conan Doyle: A Study Guide *

"A Room with a View" by E. M. Forster: A Study Guide

"Looking for Alaska" by John Green: A Study Guide

"Paper Towns" by John Green: A Study Guide

"On the Road" by Jack Keruoac: A Study Guide

"The Secret Life of Bees" by Sue Monk Kidd: A Study Guide

"An Inspector Calls" by J.B. Priestley: A Study Guide

"Macbeth" by William Shakespeare: A Study Guide *

"Othello" by William Shakespeare: A Study Guide *

"Antigone" by Sophocles: A Study Guide *

"Oedipus Rex" by Sophocles: A Study Guide

"Cannery Row" by John Steinbeck: A Study Guide

"Of Mice and Men" by John Steinbeck: A Study Guide *

"Unbroken by Laura Hillenbrand: A Study Guide

Study Guides available as e-books:

"Heart of Darkness" by Joseph Conrad: A Study Guide

"The Mill on the Floss" by George Eliot: A Study Guide

"Lord of the Flies" by William Golding: A Study Guide

"Catch-22" by Joseph Heller: A Study Guide

"Life of Pi" by Yann Martel: A Study Guide

"Nineteen Eighty-Four by George Orwell: A Study Guide

"Selected Poems" by Sylvia Plath: A Study Guide

"Henry IV Part 2" by William Shakespeare: A Study Guide

"Julius Caesar" by William Shakespeare: A Study Guide

"The Pearl" by John Steinbeck: A Study Guide

"Slaughterhouse-Five" by Kurt Vonnegut: A Study Guide

"The Bridge of San Luis Rey" by Thornton Wilder: A Study Guide

Teacher resources: Ray also publishes many more study guides and other resources for classroom use on the 'Teachers Pay Teachers' website: **http://www.teacherspayteachers.com/Store/Raymond-Moore**

Manufactured by Amazon.ca
Bolton, ON